Cl. 19.95

20013176
gr 4-8
MACARTHUR
MS

# RWANDA

# MAJOR WORLD NATIONS

# RWANDA

J.K. Pomeray

## CHELSEA HOUSE PUBLISHERS
Philadelphia

**Chelsea House Publishers**

Copyright © 2000 by Chelsea House Publishers,
a division of Main Line Book Co.

First Printing.

1  3  5  7  9  8  6  4  2


Library of Congress Cataloging-in-Publication Data

Pomeray, J. K.
Rwanda / J. K. Pomeray.
p.   cm. — (Major world nations)
Includes index.
Summary: An overview of the history, geography, economy, government,
people, and culture of the African nation of Rwanda.
ISBN 0-7910-4765-2
1. Rwanda Juvenile literature. [1. Rwanda.] I. Title.
II. Series.
DT450.14.P66   1999
967.571—dc21      99-35494
CIP

# CONTENTS

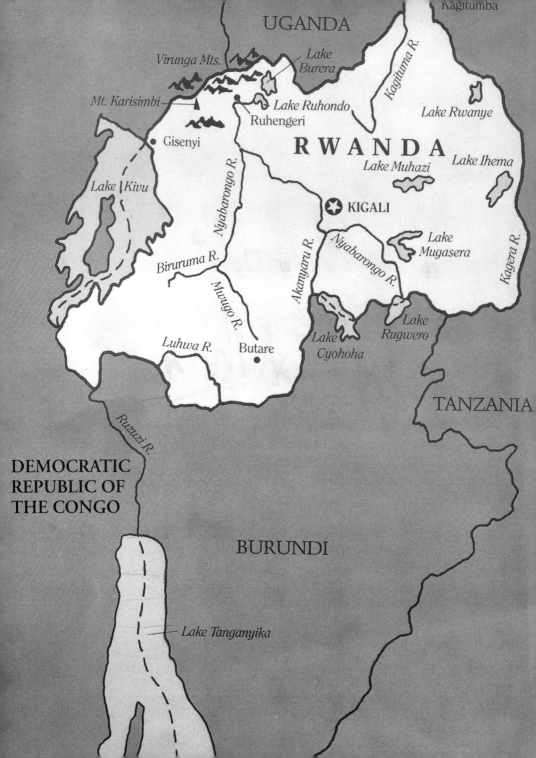

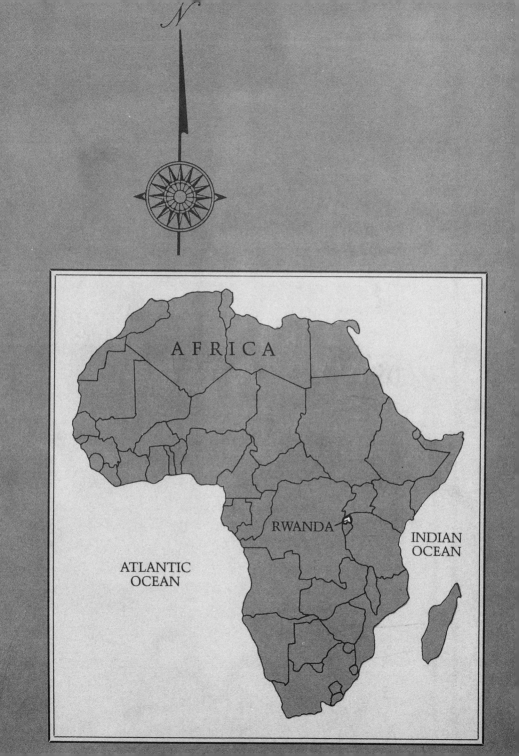

# FACTS AT A GLANCE

## Land and People

| | |
|---|---|
| **Official Name** | Rwandese Republic |
| **Location** | Central Africa |
| **Area** | 10,169 square miles (26,338 square kilometers) |
| **Climate** | Temperate |
| **Capital** | Kigali |
| **Other Cities** | Gisenyi, Ruhengeri, Butare |
| **Population** | 7,957,000 |
| **Population Density** | 590 people per square mile (228 per square kilometer) |
| **Major Lakes** | Kivu, Burera, Ruhondo, Rwanye, Muhazi, Ihema, Mugesera |
| **Major Rivers** | Kagera, Ruzizi, Kagitumba, Nyabarongo |
| **Highest Point** | Mount Karisimbi, 14,870 feet (4,532 meters) |
| **Official Languages** | Kinyarwanda, French, English |
| **Other Language** | Swahili |

8

| | |
|---|---|
| **Ethnic Groups** | Hutu, 80 percent; Tutsi, 19 percent; Twa, 1 percent |
| **Religions** | Roman Catholic, 65 percent; Protestant, 9 percent; Muslim, 1 percent; traditional religions, 18 percent |
| **Literacy Rate** | 60.5 percent |
| **Average Life Expectancy** | Males, 41.5 years; females, 42.4 years |

## Economy

| | |
|---|---|
| **Division of Labor Force** | Agriculture, 93 percent; government and services, 5 percent; industry and commerce, 2 percent |
| **Agricultural Products** | Bananas, coffee, tea, beans, peas, sweet potatoes, cassava, potatoes, corn, sorghum, peanuts |
| **Industries** | Textiles, wood, paper, processed food, rubber, plastic, mining (tin and tungsten ore) |
| **Major Imports** | Food products, machinery and equipment, steel, construction materials |
| **Major Exports** | Coffee, 74 percent; tea |
| **Currency** | Rwanda franc |

## Government

| | |
|---|---|
| **Form of Government** | Republic with executive, legislative, and judicial branches |
| **Government Bodies** | Transitional National Assembly |
| **Formal Head of State** | President |
| **Head of Government** | Prime minister |
| **Voting Rights** | All adult men and women over the age of 18 |

# HISTORY AT A GLANCE

| | |
|---|---|
| **before 1300s** A.D. | Rwanda is inhabited by the Twa, forest-dwelling hunters-gatherers. The Hutu, a more aggressive Bantu people, migrate into Rwanda from the north. |
| **by 1300s** | Many small Hutu kingdoms are established. Each kingdom centers around a family clan. |
| **1300s-1400s** | Small groups of the Tutsi people migrate into Rwanda from the Nile River basin. Although the Hutu outnumber the Tutsi, the Tutsi, who are warriors and cattle herders, gradually gain political and economic power. |
| **late 1400s** | King Ruganzu I Bwimba begins expanding Rwandan territory. |
| **mid-1500s** | King Mihamhwe I Mutbazi centralizes the monarchy and establishes the country's feudal system. |
| **late 1800s** | King Kigeri IV establishes Rwanda's present-day borders. European explorers pass near the kingdom of Rwanda but do not enter it. |
| **1885** | The Conference of Berlin gives Germany colonial rights to Rwanda. Great Britain and Belgium argue over Rwanda's borders with their neighboring colonies. |

| 1894 | German explorer Count von Gotzen is the first European to enter Rwanda. |
|---|---|
| 1907 | Explorer and scientist Richard Kandt is named the first German governor of the colony. |
| 1910 | Germany, Great Britain, and Belgium settle their border disputes. Rwanda officially becomes German territory. |
| 1912 | German soldiers help the mwami (king) put down a rebellion among the Hutu tribespeople in the northeast. |
| 1916 | During World War I, Belgian forces take over Rwanda. |
| 1923 | The League of Nations assigns Rwanda and neighboring Burundi to Belgian administration. The new territory is called Ruanda-Urundi. The Belgians reduce the mwami's power and dismantle the feudal system. |
| 1931 | The Belgians dethrone King Musinga, who goes into exile in the Congo. Belgium appoints a new king. |
| 1946 | Rwanda and Burundi become a trust territory of the United Nations, under Belgian administration. Belgium is told to prepare the Rwandans for self-government. |
| 1953 | Rwanda's first elections for advisory councils give some political power to the Hutu people. |
| 1956 | All adult men receive the right to vote in council elections. |
| late 1950s | Hutu political parties form and urge the end of Tutsi domination. |

| 1959 | Fighting breaks out between the Hutu and the Tutsi. Thousands of people are killed or forced to flee into other countries. |
|---|---|
| 1961 | Elections for a new legislature are held. The Hutu win a majority of the seats. Gregoire Kayibanda, a Hutu leader, is elected president of the new republic. |
| 1962 | The United Nations separates Rwanda and Burundi. Belgian administration ends and the Republic of Rwanda is born. |
| 1960s | Conflict continues between the Hutu and the Tutsi. Rwanda and Burundi dissolve their trade and diplomatic agreements. |
| 1965 and 1969 | Kayibanda is reelected president. The Tutsi are victims of discrimination and violence. Many Hutu form rival political groups and fight among themselves. |
| 1973 | Major General Juvenal Habyarimana, the defense minister, overthrows Kayibanda's government. He dissolves the legislature, suspends the constitution, and places the country under military rule. |
| 1975 | Habyarimana declares that the National Revolutionary Movement for Development (MRND) is the only legal political party. |
| 1978 | Habyarimana is elected president. |
| 1983 | Habyarimana is reelected president for a second consecutive term. |
| late 1980s | Habyarimana rules Rwanda without opposition and maintains close economic links with Belgium. |
| 1990 | In October Rwanda is invaded by a Tutsi military group, the Rwandan Patriotic Front (RPF). The |

Rwandan government fights off the attack and goes on a rampage against the Tutsi in the country, killing thousands and arresting thousands more.

1991-1992    The RPF invades again, this time working its way to within a few miles of the capital city. A cease-fire is called and negotiations begin but quickly stall. An all out offensive is again launched by the RPF.

1994    Habyarimana is killed when his plane is shot down. In retaliation his followers begin one of the worst massacres of the 20th century—they kill almost a million Tutsi and force millions more to flee the country.

1995    The RPF beat back the military responsible for the genocide and gain control of the country. Nearly two million refugees remain in camps in Zaire, Burundi, and Tanzania. A commission is set up to arrest and try the persons responsible for the massacre and the jails fill up. Many of the perpetrators flee the country and cannot be caught.

1996-1997    The refugees finally begin to return to Rwanda and the task of caring for all of them begins.

13

A Rwandan man carts a load of green bananas to market in Kigali. Rwandan farmers earn a small income from selling bananas and other crops they cannot use.

# 1

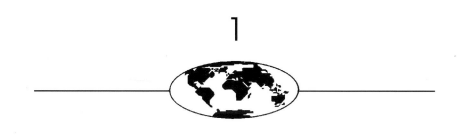

# Rwanda and the World

The Republic of Rwanda is a young nation with a long history. A newly independent, undeveloped country, Rwanda is similar to many other developing nations in Africa, where new ideas and old traditions often clash on the road to economic and social progress.

Rwanda is a tiny, landlocked nation in the heart of east central Africa. It is bordered to the north by Uganda, to the east by Tanzania, to the south by Burundi, and to the west by the Democratic Republic of the Congo (Zaire). The Indian Ocean lies more than 700 miles (1,126 kilometers) to the east.

Rwanda became an independent country just 37 years ago, but its history dates back much earlier. Rwanda's first inhabitants, the Twa, settled in the region 35,000 years ago. Other peoples—the Hutu and the Tutsi—settled there between the 7th and 15th centuries A.D. These tribal groups lived primarily by hunting, farming, and cattle herding. Many of their traditional practices continue today. Farming with hand-held hoes is still the main occupation of most Rwandans. Belief in the spirit world of sacred gods and ancestors still pervades their religions. And the traditional language, Kinyarwanda, is one of three official languages in the republic along with French and English.

These customs have endured through different eras of Rwandan history, such as the period between the 15th and 19th centuries. During this era, the Tutsi dominated the majority Hutu through a powerful, highly centralized feudal system. But despite their social, political, and economic differences, the Hutu and Tutsi shared a common language, religion, and artistic pursuits.

In the late 1800s, the kingdom of Rwanda was colonized—first by Germany, then by Belgium. The Europeans treated the kingdom of Rwanda and the neighboring kingdom of Burundi as one colonial territory. Although the two regions had significant similarities—including their peoples, cultures, and Tutsi-dominated feudal systems—their differences were stronger. For centuries before colonization, Rwanda and Burundi had violently disputed their borders.

The colonists tried to develop Rwanda's economy and political system, as well as to set up education and health-care programs. Although these efforts succeeded in other colonies, they never developed to the extent planned in Rwanda. Transportation systems to handle trade were insufficient or nonexistent, and educational programs reached relatively few people.

Colonial development did, however, break up the Tutsi-dominated feudal system. An organized Hutu movement for independence then arose in Rwanda and Burundi. The movement gained momentum more quickly in Rwanda, because Rwanda's government was more organized. Just before independence, government officials agreed that these political differences, as well as longtime tribal hostilities, prevented Rwanda and Burundi from becoming one united, independent nation. As a result, each became an independent republic.

Although the independence movement succeeded, conflicts between the Hutu and the Tutsi continued in Rwanda. In 1973, political unrest led to a military coup in which Juvenal Habyarimana gained control of the country. Habyarimana's government stabilized Rwanda's internal conflicts. It also improved relations with Burundi, its longtime rival, and signed political and

**The terraced fields that end abruptly at the border with the Democratic Republic of the Congo graphically demonstrate the limited amount of land available for farming in Rwanda.**

economic agreements with that country and with Zaire, now the Democratic Republic of the Congo.

Despite foreign assistance, Rwanda lacks money for social and economic development. Firmly entrenched traditional ways make development slow as does the conflict between the tribes.

Lack of communication and transportation networks (there is still no railroad) keeps the rural areas isolated and remote. It is difficult to introduce more advanced farming techniques and to establish hospitals and schools.

**Schoolchildren leave their one-room schoolhouse and head for the gates of their family compound, or *rugo*. Lashed branches form the boundaries of the *rugo*.**

Rwanda has many farms but little land that can be used for farming. The fertile areas are, therefore, the most densely populated and they tend to suffer from erosion caused by over planting and overgrazing. Rwanda's erratic climate also contributes to lower crop yields, which has worsened the problems of overcrowding, malnutrition, and poverty. Moreover, the population is growing at an extremely high rate.

While these problems have persisted in Rwanda, some other African nations have achieved economic and social progress. Despite certain concessions to modernization the majority of Rwandans live in the same place and in the same way that their fathers and forefathers did. Although there is a small, educated elite and a somewhat larger pool of skilled workers, most Rwandans earn their living by tilling the soil on which they live, just as they have done for centuries. Like the land itself, they remain largely unmoved and unchanged by attempts to propel them into the modern world.

War between the Tutsi and the Hutu tribes in the 1990s and the full scale massacre of the Tutsis has, of course, further setback any progress in modernization that Rwanda had made and has devastated the country.

There remains great potential for economic and social progress, but success will require many more years. Success depends on whether or not there will be compromises—between the tribes of Rwanda, and the forces of change and of ancient tradition.

This series of volcanic peaks forms the Virunga Mountains, Rwanda's only mountain range. The Virunga Mountains mark Rwanda's northwestern border with the Democratic Republic of the Congo.

# 2

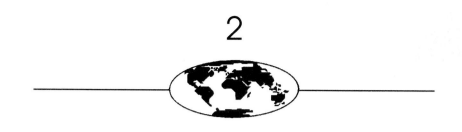

# A Land of Lakes

One of Africa's smallest nations, Rwanda covers 10,169 square miles (26,338 square kilometers), making it a little larger than the state of Maryland. The country is nicknamed "Land of a Thousand Hills" because of its generally high, sloping terrain. Yet the landscape varies significantly and can be divided into distinct geographical regions: the Great Rift Valley along the western border, the Virunga Mountains in the northwest, the Congo-Nile Crest on the eastern edge of the Great Rift Valley, the central plateaus, and the lowland swamps and savannas in the eastern border zones.

Running between Lake Kivu on the west and the Congo-Nile Crest on the east is a narrow section of Africa's Great Rift Valley. This valley is actually a vast series of valleys, canyons, lakes, and seas that extends north-to south from Jordan in the Middle East through Mozambique in southeastern Africa, and out into the Indian Ocean. Its formation began millions of years ago when extreme pressure beneath the earth's crust created a rift, or large crack, in its surface. Continued pressure along this rift caused some areas of the land to cave in, creating valleys, while other areas piled up to form mountain ridges and peaks.

Over the centuries, volcanic eruptions and widespread erosion further molded and changed the face of the land. Some of the valleys filled in with water. Lake Kivu was formed in this way, as was Lake Tanganyika to the south and the Red Sea between Egypt and Saudi Arabia.

The Great Rift Valley contains some of Rwanda's highest elevations, with altitudes ranging from 2,600 feet (793 meters) to 6,000 feet (1,829 meters) above sea level. It also supports many farms, particularly in the northern part of the valley, where rich volcanic soils yield good crops.

In the northwest corner of Rwanda, at the Democratic Republic of the Congo (Zaire) border, lies a series of volcanic peaks known as the Virunga Mountains. These mountains resulted from the tremendous upheavals that occurred in the Great Rift Valley centuries ago. Five of the peaks lie within Rwanda, and three within the Democratic Republic of the Congo (Zaire). Two of these former volcanoes still emit smoke and steam. The tallest of the Virunga peaks, Mount Karisimbi, rises to 14,870 feet (4,532 meters) above sea level in Rwanda.

Even though the Virunga Mountains are less than 100 miles (161 kilometers) from the equator, the highest peaks are snow-capped year round. The upper elevations are too cold for trees, but lush rain forests cover the lower and middle mountain slopes. Just south of the Virunga Mountains are the high lava plains. Rich

**Smoke and steam still vent from some of the volcanic peaks in the Virunga Mountains. The peaks reach heights of more than 14,000 feet (4,000 meters).**

in volcanic soil, this is one of Rwanda's most agriculturally productive regions.

On the eastern edge of the Great Rift Valley, the land rises sharply in a series of dramatic ridges. These ridges form the western slopes of the Congo-Nile Crest, also known as the Nile-Congo divide. This mountainous ridge is the dividing point, or watershed, between Africa's two greatest river systems—the Nile and the Congo. From here, the two rivers begin their long, winding journeys through Africa to the sea, the Nile flowing north to the Mediterranean Sea, the Congo west to the Atlantic Ocean.

On the western slopes, heavy rains feed short, twisted rivers and streams that rush down to the Nile and Congo basins. Periodic flooding causes serious soil erosion. Much of the natural vegetation has been cleared for farming, which makes erosion even worse. The remaining vegetation consists of grasslands and gallery forest—tracts of large trees that form a canopy over open corridors on the forest floor below.

The granite-based soils in the higher elevations of the Congo-Nile Crest support most of Rwanda's remaining forests. The peaks of the crest form a band from 12 to 30 miles (19 to 48 kilometers) wide. They average about 9,000 feet (2,743 meters) above sea level, but some peaks reach to almost 10,000 feet (3,048 meters).

From the eastern slopes of the Congo-Nile Crest, the central plateaus stretch toward the lowlands of the eastern border. The plateaus are actually a series of rolling hills that become gradually lower as they move eastward.

Once covered in great forests, this land is now almost all cleared for farming and cattle grazing. Centuries of intensive farming and grazing have caused serious erosion and soil depletion. To help conserve the soil, the Rwandan government has built thousands of miles of hedges and small dikes.

The rolling hills of the central plateau gradually slope off into the swamps and savannas of eastern Rwanda. (Savannas are grassy plains with scattered thorny bushes and low, scrubby

**The Kagera River rushes through a range of high, rounded hills that overlook Rwanda's border with Tanzania. Many other rivers and lakes cover the Rwandan countryside.**

trees.) This region is green and lush after heavy rains, but becomes brown and parched during dry spells. Brush fires and overgrazing by cattle have destroyed much of the savannas. The southeastern part of Rwanda is filled with lakes and marshes.

Rwanda is a land of many rivers and lakes, some of which form its borders with neighboring countries. The Kagera River marks the eastern boundary with Tanzania and part of the southern boundary with Burundi. Sections of the Rwanda-Burundi border are also formed by Lake Rugwero, Lake Cyohoha, and the Akanyaru and Luhwa rivers.

25

Most of the western border with the Democratic Republic of the Congo (Zaire) is formed by Lake Kivu and the Ruzizi River, which drains into Lake Tanganyika on the Democratic Republic of the Congo (Zaire)-Burundi border. Lake Kivu is Rwanda's largest body of water. At an elevation of 4,700 feet (1,433 meters), its waters are cool and clear, although fish life is discouraged by a high concentration of poisonous methane gas, which seeps up from the bottom of the lake and dissolves in the water. On Lake Kivu's northeastern shore lies the town of Gisenyi, Rwanda's major resort area. Visitors enjoy its pleasant beaches, many small islands, and lush vegetation set against a background of high mountains.

In Rwanda's northeast corner, the Kagitumba River forms a small portion of the Rwanda-Uganda border. The border town of Kagitumba sits at the junction of the Kagitumba and Kagera rivers.

Eight large lakes lie completely within Rwanda's borders: Burera and Ruhondo in the northern mountains, near the Ugandan border, and Rwanye, Hago, Muhazi, Ihema, Mugesera, and Rwehikama in the eastern part of the country. All of these lakes teem with fish.

Most of Rwanda's interior rivers and streams connect with the beginnings of the Nile and Congo rivers. In fact, some authorities claim that the actual source of the Nile River is a tributary of the Mwogo River high in Rwanda's Congo-Nile Crest.

To the east of the Congo-Nile Crest, in an area sometimes called the Kagera Basin, lie the Nyabarongo River and its main tribu-

26

A mother mountain gorilla nurses her child in the northern rain forest.

taries, the Mwogo, Lukarara, Biruruma, Mukungwa, Base, Nyabugogo, and Akanyaru rivers. These rivers flow southward and eastward from the central plateaus and from the eastern lakes and swamps into the Kagera River. The Kagera flows northward and passes through Tanzania on its way into Lake Victoria, one of the major sources of the mighty Nile. The lake is bordered by Tanzania, Uganda, and Kenya.

On the western slopes of the Congo-Nile Crest, many small

mountain streams flow into Lake Kivu or the Ruzizi River valley. Lake Kivu drains into the Ruzizi, which flows swiftly southward into Lake Tanganyika to join with the streams that form the Congo River.

Although located only two degrees south of the equator, Rwanda has a relatively mild and pleasant climate. It's overall high elevation makes temperatures cooler than those of most tropical areas.

In the central plateau region, average daily temperatures range from about 65 degrees Fahrenheit (19 degrees Celsius) to 75 degrees Fahrenheit (22 degrees Celsius). In the mountains to the

**Two armed game wardens at the National Park of Volcanoes display their equipment.**

west and north, the weather is much cooler, with night temperatures dropping to below freezing in the higher elevations. Eastward, temperatures become hotter as elevations decrease, averaging about 90 degrees Fahrenheit (32 degrees Celsius) in the northeastern grasslands and southeastern swamps.

Rainfall varies according to elevation as well. Some of the highest elevations in the Congo-Nile Crest may receive more than 70 inches (1,788 millimeters) per year, whereas the lower lands to the east may get only 30 inches (762 millimeters). This pattern can change from year to year and even from month to month. Unevenly alternating periods of prolonged, heavy rainfall and extreme droughts are also common. This is especially true in the central and eastern parts of the country, where up to 30 inches (762 millimeters) of rain may fall all at once.

Generally, Rwanda has two dry seasons—the short season in January and February and the long season from June through September. It also has two wet seasons, from March through May and from October through December.

Rwanda's varied terrain and numerous water sources attract beautiful, exotic wildlife. Lions, cheetahs, elephants, buffalo, zebras, giraffes, hyenas, warthogs, gazelles, antelope, and rhinoceroses roam the savannas. Hippopotamuses, crocodiles, fish, and reptiles thrive in the lakes, rivers, and swamps. Rain forests shelter the rare mountain gorilla and other primates, and are home to the python and cobra.

However, advancing human settlements have driven out or destroyed hundreds of species of animals, reptiles, birds, and fish.

In the last 100 years alone, 67 species of mammals have vanished. Today, Rwanda's most endangered mammals include the cheetah, white rhinoceros, and mountain gorilla.

In recent decades, Rwanda has established two large conservation areas to protect its wildlife. One is Akagera National Park in eastern Rwanda. It covers about 1,000 square miles (2,560 square kilometers), which is almost one-tenth of the country's total land area. The park's savannas provided a protected habitat for an estimated half-million wild animals but the recent civil war seriously depleted these numbers. Rwandan law preserves the park's land and restricts hunting on the premises and hopefully the wildlife will be restored.

Game wardens constantly patrol the park to guard against illegal hunters or poachers. These poachers are the park's biggest problem. Besides the few who kill protected game for food, many poachers hunt the rare and most valuable species, such as the leopard and the rhinoceros. Leopard skins and rhinoceros horn bring the poachers a high price in illegal sales.

Rwanda's other game preserve and conservation area is the National Park of the Volcanoes in northwestern Rwanda. It is named for the volcanic Virunga Mountains that stretch through the heart of the park. The preserve borders the Democratic Republic of the Congo (Zaire) and continues into that country.

Roaming through the preserve's lush rain forests are rare mountain gorillas, the largest of all apes. An adult male may stand six feet (1.8 meters) tall and weigh more than 400 pounds (181 kilograms). Mountain gorillas live in groups remarkably like the traditional extended families of humans. A patriarch, or male head of the family, leads the group and is usually the largest and strongest gorilla. The others in the group—females, subordinate males, and the young—all recognize his leadership. The group lives, travels, and forages for food together; they also communicate in a complex language of sounds and gestures. Despite their large size and menacing appearance, mountain gorillas are actually gentle, timid vegetarians.

Once, tens of thousands of mountain gorillas lived in Rwanda. However, poachers and encroaching Tutsi herdsmen have decimated their numbers so that only a few hundred remain; they live in protected isolation in national preserves.

Rwanda was traditionally ruled by a *mwami* (king). This photograph shows one of the most powerful Rwandan kings, Yuhi Musinga, meeting with his headmen.

# 3

# From Kingdom to Colony

Rwandan history was first recorded by Europeans who explored the east central region of Africa in the late 1800s. But tribal folklore and archaeological studies recount a much earlier history.

The first people known to have lived in the area of present-day Rwanda are the Twa. They are related to the Pygmies, the first inhabitants of east central Africa. Archaeological records indicate that the Twa settled in Rwanda as far back as 35,000 years ago. Forest-dwellers who hunted and gathered wild foods such as fruit, nuts, and roots, the Twa eventually moved deep into the forests to flee the Hutu, the next group of people who settled Rwanda.

The Hutu are believed to have migrated to Rwanda from the Bantu lands to the north between the 7th and 10th centuries A.D. By the 15th century they had established many small farming kingdoms in Rwanda. Each kingdom centered around a particular family clan ruled by a king known as a *bahinza*, "he who causes things to grow." The Hutu revered the bahinza, believing he had magical powers to make rain and protect their crops and cattle.

Next to arrive in Rwanda were the Tutsi, a tall, proud people who slowly migrated from their Nile River basin homelands between the 14th and 15th centuries. The Tutsi were fierce warriors who owned large herds of cattle. They were esteemed by the Hutu because, in the traditional African society, warfare determined strength and cattle represented wealth.

The Tutsi's sense of pride and nobility sprang from more than skilled fighting and cattle ownership. The Tutsi claimed the gods had chosen them to rule the Hutu, who far outnumbered them. This claim stemmed from the Tutsi legend of three children born in "the north" (the Tutsi equivalent of heaven): two brothers, Kigwa and Mututsi, and a sister, Nyampundu. One day the three children accidentally fell to earth, bringing with them fire, iron, the forge, and cattle. Once on earth, Kigwa and Nyampundu married and formed the first Tutsi clan, the Abanyiginya. One of the descendants of this clan, Gilhanga (whose name means "founder"), first led the Tutsi into Rwanda and established a settlement between Lake Muhazi and Lake Mugesera. Later, according to the legend, Gilhanga's son Kanyaruanda became Rwanda's first *mwami*, or "king."

In reality, the Tutsi conquest of Rwanda followed several centuries of fighting, mostly between Tutsi and Hutu but also between rival Tutsi families. Frequent conflicts with Tutsi clans from the neighboring kingdom of Burundi created a hostility between the two nations that exists to this day.

After the Tutsi conquered most of Rwanda, the Tutsi mwami took over Hutu land, giving his people social, economic, and political superiority over the Hutu. The Tutsi ruled Rwanda for several centuries; the Hutu retained control of only small areas in northeastern Rwanda during this period.

Strength and prosperity enabled the Tutsi to dominate the Hutu. To maintain power, the Tutsi gradually implemented a feudal system, known as *ubuhake*, in which they were the ruling class, or aristocracy. Hutu peasants pledged themselves to a Tutsi lord, exchanging their crops and labor for the protection and use of the lord's land and cattle. The peasants worked the lord's fields, repaired his houses, cared for his cattle, and served in his army. The lord was thus freed from all manual labor. When a lord or peasant died, his son inherited his ubuhake obligations.

Not all ubuhake arrangements were between Tutsi and Hutu. Less powerful Tutsi frequently pledged themselves to richer and stronger Tutsi lords. They did not perform physical labor, but provided important military support for the lords during their military campaigns.

The Tutsi capital was Nyanza. From here the mwami ruled the kingdom of Rwanda. According to legend, the mwami was the descendant of divine spirits and "the eye through which God

**Cattle have played an extremely important role in Rwandan society.**

looks upon Rwanda." His royal symbol of power was the *kalinga*, or "sacred drum."

The mwami appointed a council of "great chiefs" to advise him on important matters. Each great chief supervised a district within the kingdom. Each district was divided into *umusozi*, or "hills," each of which was administered by a hill chief. The umusozi were further divided into neighborhoods directed by subchiefs. Military chiefs carried out cattle raids on neighboring groups and protected the borders against invaders.

In each district, a cattle chief and a land chief collected the tribute—cattle and farm produce—owed to the mwami. The mwami would keep the cattle and crops he wanted; he would then distribute the rest to his favorite chiefs and subchiefs. The most powerful families competed for the mwami's favor as well as for the prestige of the chieftaincies. This helped to assure the loyalty of the mwami's subjects and the continued strength of the ubuhake system.

The mwami's court also contained *biru,* the Tutsi "guardians of tradition." The biru advised the mwami on spiritual matters, interpreted tribal history, performed court rituals, and, with the guidance of the spirits, helped select the mwami's successor. The biru were vital to the Tutsi monarchial system because they supported the traditions that held that the Tutsi were the god-appointed, predestined rulers of the Hutu.

Rwandan oral tradition honors many great *bami* (the plural of mwami). Mwami Ruganzu I Bwimba, who ruled at the end of the 15th century, began Rwanda's first period of expansion. Mwami

36

Mibambwe I Mutbazi centralized the monarchy and solidified the feudal system in the mid-16th century. Mwami Kigeri IV established Rwanda's approximate present-day borders in the late 19th century.

For centuries the bami ruled virtually unchallenged by internal or external forces. But in the late 1800s, Europeans began to colonize east central Africa as they discovered its abundant riches and fertile lands. With the colonists came new ideas that challenged old traditions.

Until a century ago, the kingdom of Rwanda was isolated from most of the world. Its remote location and the fierce reputation of the Tutsi warriors discouraged outsiders from entering Rwanda.

**The famous British-American explorer, Sir Henry Stanley, passed through northern Rwanda in the 1870s.**

This isolation greatly benefitted Rwandans. Unlike many of their neighbors, they were not forced into slavery by Arab slave traders. Periodically, Arabs tried to penetrate the kingdom, but skilled Tutsi warriors always drove them off.

Rwanda was one of the last areas of Africa reached by Europeans, who referred to it as Ruanda. In 1855, British explorers Sir Richard Burton and John Hanning Speke traveled near Rwanda to seek the source of the Nile River, but they never entered the kingdom. In 1861, Speke again ventured near the Rwandan border on his trip to Lake Victoria. The famous explorer Henry Morton Stanley passed through the northeastern frontier in 1876 but did not enter the interior.

As exploration of east central Africa continued, European nations disputed one another's rights to colonize the region. In 1885, European nations met at the Conference of Berlin to settle these arguments by dividing the region among European powers. The kingdoms of Rwanda and Burundi (known as Urundi to the Europeans) were assigned to Germany. In 1894, German explorer Count von Gotzen was the first European to traverse Rwanda. On this mission, he discovered Lake Kivu and met Mwami Kigeri IV.

Germany, Belgium, and Great Britain failed to agree on the territorial borders set at the Berlin Conference—especially those around Rwanda and Burundi, which lay at the strategic meeting place of the three colonial empires. Britain saw the territory as a necessary link in a railway system that could unite Britain's northern and southern African colonies. Belgium, which controlled the

Congo Free State (now the Democratic Republic of the Congo), wanted Rwanda and Burundi because they linked the Congo with Lake Victoria and the east coast of Africa. And Germany wanted to make the region part of German East Africa, an empire that already included Tanganyika (now Tanzania).

To establish claims in Rwanda and Burundi, Germany installed a military post at Bujumbura (known as Usumbura to the Europeans) in western Burundi in 1897. In 1898, the Germans joined the two kingdoms into one administrative territory, known as Ruanda-Urundi. In 1907, the Germans appointed Ruanda-Urundi's first resident colonial governor, a prominent explorer and scientist named Dr. Richard Kandt.

**One legacy of colonial government was the introduction of church-sponsored schools.**

At the same time, Germany, Great Britain, and Belgium were still disputing their colonies' borders. In 1910, they finally agreed to permanent boundaries and Ruanda-Urundi officially became Germany's possession.

Both Rwanda and Burundi were ruled by Tutsi kings who headed feudal systems. But feudalism was much stricter in Rwanda, and Rwanda's mwami had more power than his Burundian counterpart. Recognizing this, the Germans worked with the Tutsi mwami and the traditional feudal system; their influence over the less powerful monarchy in Burundi was more limited.

Working with the traditional Rwandan system benefitted both the Germans and the ruling Rwandans. The German administration was able to operate with only a small number of colonists, and the mwami was able to use German troops and influence to strengthen his own position.

This policy proved especially helpful to the mwami when dealing with rebellious Hutu clans in Rwanda s northeastern border sections. In 1912, Mwami Yuhi Musinga sent an expedition of German soldiers to squelch a Hutu rebellion in the northeast. During the period of German colonization, Musinga came closer than any of his predecessors to gaining control over all of Rwanda.

After the Germans abolished most of the traditional chieftaincies (land and cattle chiefs, hill chiefs), the mwami ruled his people directly. The Germans also took a census of the population, imposed a tax on each Rwandan, and introduced coffee as a cash crop. The German administration started to replace the tradition-

40

al barter, or trading, system with a money economy to handle foreign currency earned by coffee exports.

German missionaries set up schools to educate Tutsi children. A few Hutu children were also accepted into the schools, which gave them a chance to improve their standing in Rwandan society. Eventually, some educated Hutu were able to get jobs in the German administration and marry into Tutsi families.

World War I interrupted Germany's plans for further developing Ruanda-Urundi and its other African territories. In Africa, Germany's forces were far outnumbered by those of its enemies, particularly Belgium. In the spring of 1916, Belgian forces advanced on Ruanda-Urundi. They met little resistance from the small German garrisons there, and by May 1916, the territory was under Belgian control.

But the Belgians did not intend to keep the territory. After the war was over, they hoped to trade it for some land near the Congo River to add to their Congo empire. But the exchange never happened. In 1923, the League of Nations gave Belgium a mandate to supervise Ruanda-Urundi.

The League's mandate meant that the Belgians were responsible for maintaining peace, order, and efficient government in the territory. They were supposed to set up modern health and education programs, as well as promote economic and social progress.

At first, the Belgians followed the German model in governing Ruanda-Urundi, retaining the Tutsi monarchy and the feudal social structure. But later they limited the power of the mwami and dismantled the ubuhake system. These changes were intended to reduce the Tutsi power over the Hutu so that both peoples could enjoy the same rights and privileges. They were also meant to stimulate economic growth, which had been held back by feudalism.

Mwami Musinga resisted these changes. In 1931, the Belgian administration deposed Musinga and exiled him to the Congo, where he remained until his death in 1940. The Belgians also broke tradition by not consulting the biru on the selection of the new mwami. Instead, they named Musinga's 18-year-old son, Charles Mutara III Rudahibwa, the new king. In 1943, they took another step toward broadening political participation and power. Lower chief councils were established throughout the kingdom to advise the mwami and his great chiefs. The mwami appointed members, who were then approved by the Belgian administration.

The Belgians tried to make Ruanda-Urundi more economically self-sufficient by increasing the production of staple foods. They also planted more coffee for export and introduced modern farming methods. These methods helped prevent the periodic famines that had plagued Rwanda for so long. The Belgians expanded the school system started by the Germans. In addition to training the sons of Tutsi chiefs for government positions, the Catholic mission schools began to offer primary education for almost all Rwandan children. This educational policy was part of Belgium's effort to create a more egalitarian society—one in which all peoples shared the same rights and privileges.

This effort took on new emphasis after World War II, when the League of Nations was replaced by a new international organization, the United Nations (UN). In 1946, Ruanda-Urundi became a UN Trust Territory under Belgian administration. The UN still required Belgium to work for the continued economic progress and well-being of the people, but it also ordered Belgium to prepare Ruanda-Urundi for eventual self-government and independence. Many Tutsi resisted this plan because they feared they would lose their wealth and power to the Hutu majority if feudalism were abolished. Despite their opposition, however, Rwanda was on its way to becoming an independent republic.

Rwanda is one of Africa's most underdeveloped nations and depends heavily on foreign assistance. This grain-storage building was built with American aid.

# 4

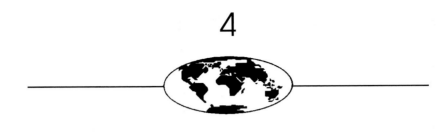

# Road to Independence

Ruanda-Urundi remained a United Nations (UN) Trust Territory for 13 years. During this time, the UN and Belgium often disagreed on how to run the country. Belgium wanted to concentrate on economic and social development because it felt that worthwhile political change could come only after the country's many economic and social problems had been resolved. The UN wanted immediate political change along with social and economic progress.

In the early 1950s, the UN Trusteeship Council pressured Belgium for swifter political change. In response, Belgium enacted some important reforms that broadened the people's participation in government. The decree of July 14, 1952, called for limited elections for the lower councils that advised the mwami and his great chiefs. This broke the tradition of councils appointed by the mwami. The first elections, held in 1953, also established the High Council of State, the most powerful branch of the government. Headed by the mwami, the High Council consisted of chiefs as well as Belgian administrators. The 1953 vote gave the

Tutsi control over all the councils, but the Hutu won enough council seats to give them a significant role in government for the first time.

In 1954, the High Council decided to abolish the ubuhake system gradually. Over the next four years, about 200,000 head of cattle were redistributed among the people, mostly the Hutu. Although the Tutsi kept most of the pastureland (and thus maintained dominance over the Hutu), the end of the ubuhake system eventually changed the pattern of life in Ruanda-Urundi. With land ownership, positions in government, and schooling open to them, the Hutu began to believe that equality was possible.

Another large step toward equality came in 1956, when all adult males were given the right to vote in council elections. Many Hutu were elected to the lower councils, especially to those that represented the northern districts of the country—the traditional Hutu strongholds against Tutsi dominance. The High Council, however, remained almost exclusively Tutsi.

In February 1957, the High Council released a "Statement of Views," which called for immediate steps toward independence by preparing the country's leaders to run a modern government. Because most of these leaders were Tutsi, Hutu leaders saw the statement as a Tutsi attempt to stay in power.

Hutu leaders issued "The Manifesto of the Bahutu" the following month. Although the manifesto agreed that the people should have greater participation in government, it declared that the basic problem of the country was the political, social, and economic dominance by the Tutsi minority over the Hutu majority. The manifesto called for the continuation of UN trusteeship and Belgian administration until equality was achieved.

The manifesto inspired the Hutu to organize opposition to Tutsi rule. Hutu political organizations sprang up, including the Hutu Social Movement and the Association for the Social Betterment of the Masses (APROSOMA). Through its newspaper, *The Voice of the Common People*, APROSOMA strongly attacked the entire system of Tutsi domination. In January 1959, APROSOMA became a legitimate political party. In September of that same year, Tutsi leaders formed the moderate Ruandan Democratic Rally (RADER), which emphasized ethnic cooperation to achieve democracy. The more radical Tutsi organized the Ruanda National Union party (UNAR), which promoted the continuation of Tutsi dominance. UNAR accused the Belgian administration of encouraging Hutu uprisings and dividing the country. It also lashed out against the leaders of Hutu parties and against the moderate Tutsi of RADER.

In October, the Hutu Social movement became the Party of the Hutu Emancipation movement (PARMEHUTU). The most radical and most popular Hutu party, PARMEHUTU wanted sweep-

**Armed Hutu men watch for Tutsi traveling this road during ethnic fighting in 1959.**

ing land reforms, Hutu access to all levels of public education, and an immediate end to the feudal system and Tutsi domination. Its leader, Gregoire Kayibanda, had been one of the signers of the manifesto of the Bahutu in 1957. Echoing the manifesto, he again called for immediate steps toward true democracy.

Tensions mounted throughout the fall of 1959. In November, fighting broke out between the Hutu and the Tutsi. Hutu raided and burned nearly 5,000 Tutsi huts, and Tutsi commandos killed several APROSOMA and PARMEHUTU leaders. Before the fighting ended, thousands of people had been killed, most of them Tutsi. Thousands more Tutsi were forced to flee to other countries, such as Uganda and the Congo.

After almost two years of unrest and political turmoil, elections for the new legislative National Assembly were held in October 1961, under UN supervision. PARMEHUTU received nearly 80 percent of the vote and became the largest party in the assembly. Shortly after the elections, the assembly voted to abolish the traditional monarchy, stripping the mwami of all authority and setting up a democratic state, or republic. On October 26 Gregoire Kayibanda was elected president of the republic.

Belgium granted the new republic of Ruanda powers of self-government. In 1962, the UN General Assembly met to consider how a united government could rule all of Ruanda-Urundi. Representatives from the two territories agreed on certain issues, such as the formation of a joint monetary and customs union and a coffee board. But they argued that historical antagonisms and vastly different political situations made unification impossible.

48

**In 1964, Rwanda introduced its own currency, which bore the likeness of the president.**

The UN agreed, and voted to restore the ancient boundaries between Ruanda and Urundi.

Belgian administration officially ended on June 27, 1962, when the UN voted to end the trusteeship agreement. Three days later, on July 1, 1962, Ruanda officially became an independent nation known as the Republic of Rwanda. On that same day, Urundi became the independent Republic of Burundi.

Independence did not end the conflict between the Tutsi and

the Hutu. The defeated, Tutsi-dominated National Union of Rwanda (UNAR), whose members had been exiled in Burundi, launched guerrilla raids in Rwanda. But these attacks did not weaken PARMEHUTU power, and Hutu forces retaliated by killing many Rwandan Tutsi. During the Hutu-Tutsi conflicts from 1959 through 1964, about 12,000 Tutsi were killed, and as many as 150,000 fled the country.

Hutu-Tutsi violence led to increased hostility between Rwanda and Burundi. The Tutsi government of Burundi charged the Rwandan government with authorizing the massacre of Tutsi tribesmen. In turn, Rwanda accused Burundi of harboring and backing the UNAR guerrillas. In 1964, Rwanda dissolved its economic agreements with Burundi and introduced its own national unit of currency, the Rwanda franc.

President Gregoire Kayibanda of the PARMEHUTU was reelected in 1965 and in 1969. Although PARMEHUTU was the dominant political party during this period, the Tutsi continued to hold many prominent positions in government, education, and the Catholic church. This angered many Hutu, especially the Gitarama, a politically powerful and openly racist group from Rwanda's central plateau region.

The Gitarama gained control of the PARMEHUTU in the late 1960s, ushering in a new era of discrimination and violence against the Tutsi. Many Tutsi were expelled from their positions in schools, churches, and government and were forced to leave the country.

At the same time, regional conflict grew between rival Hutu groups. The Gitarama isolated itself from other Hutu factions, especially those in the northern provinces of Gisenyi and Ruhengeri. These areas had been the traditional strongholds of Hutu resistance against Tutsi feudal rule. Now their proud residents were excluded from participation in their own government.

Growing disunity in the PARMEHUTU government led to a military coup (overthrow of the government) on July 5, 1973. The defense minister, Major General Juvenal Habyarimana, overthrew President Kayibanda. Habyarimana, a northerner, had the backing of the military and the police, as well as those Rwandans who wished to see an end to ethnic and regional conflicts.

After the coup, Habyarimana quickly dissolved the National Assembly, suspended Rwanda's constitution, and established martial law. In 1975, he outlawed the PARMEHUTU and made his National Revolutionary Movement for Development (MNRD) the country's only political party. Without opposition, Habyarimana was elected to a five-year term as president in December 1978, and again in December 1983.

Habyarimana's rule led to reduced ethnic tension, a blurring of regional differences, and movement away from Socialist economic policies. Relations improved with Burundi, the Democratic Republic of the Congo (Zaire), and Uganda, although disruption during Idi Amin's reign of terror in Uganda (1971-1979) temporarily damaged Rwanda's economy by closing off its major trade routes to the north. And in 1982, the Ugandan government expelled about 45,000 Tutsi refugees, stealing their cattle and burning their homes. Thousands fled back to Rwanda, pleading for food and shelter.

**Refugees cross the border into Rwanda after years of exile following the 1994 massacre.**

The Habyarimana regime maintained close ties with Belgium. Belgian advisors and consultants held important positions in the Rwandan army and government. Belgium remained Rwanda's major source of economic aid, and Belgians controlled much of its industry, particularly mining and manufacturing.

Although the Habyarimana regime stabilized Rwanda, it was charged with restricting civil and political rights. For example, Rwandans could not live wherever they wanted to—the government restricted internal movement to prevent mass migrations from rural to urban areas. And although all citizens have the right to vote, their choice was limited to candidates from Habyarimana's party. Because of these restrictions, the United Nations did not consider Rwanda a free country.

However, the Habyarimana regime tolerated and sometimes

even encouraged political criticism voiced through the press (although all newspapers were subject to censorship by the Ministry of Information). It generally respected freedom of religion and the right to assemble.

Rwanda was accused of serious human rights violations, such as jailing persons for long periods of time without formal charges, and torturing prisoners. (Many of these prisoners once held high positions in the Kayibanda regime.) In January 1980, President Habyarimana signed a more lenient penal code designed to reduce these and other violations.

In October 1990 Rwanda was invaded by a Tutsi military group based in Uganda, the Rwandan Patriotic Front (RPF). Habyarimana requested foreign help in fighting off the attack and France and Belgium as well as neighboring Zaire responded. They fought off the attack but then the Rwandan government went on a rampage against the Tutsi population and any Hutu thought to be involved. Thousands were killed and thousands of others were arrested and held without food and water. But this was not to be the worst of it.

The RPF again invaded in 1991. This time they were better armed and better prepared. By 1992 they had fought their way to only a few miles from the capital city of Kigali. A cease-fire was called and the parties met at the negotiating table. But the negotiations stalled and the RPF again launched an all-out offensive.

In 1994 Habyarimana called for a meeting of all the regional presidents. On his return trip to Kigali his plane was shot down killing both Habyarimana and the president of Burundi who had accompanied him. The incident sparked one of the worst massacres of the 20th century.

In anger, Habyarimana's supporters decided to end the Tutsi problem once and for all by exterminating them—mass genocide. The Hutu prime minister was killed, because he was too moderate, along with Belgian United Nations's peacekeeping forces. Then Colonel Bagosora, the army commander, led death squads all over the country, killing, looting, and burning. Thousands were killed every day. Millions of Tutsi fled the country.

The RPF eventually overcame the military and took over the country but the loss and damage were incredible. Estimates are that almost a million Tutsi had been killed and millions more were refugees in neighboring countries.

Eventually a legal commission was set up to try those responsible for the genocide and the jails are overflowing with those awaiting trial. But many of those responsible also fled the country.

The refugees, suffering in camps in Zaire and Tanzania, feared going home for many years because of continued unrest and threats. They only started returning in 1996 and 1997.

President Juvenal Habyarimana who held power from the 1973 coup until his death in 1994, had declared that his National Revolutionary Movement for Development (MNRD) was the only political party allowed in Rwanda.

In May of 1995 a new constitution was adopted that allowed for a multiparty system of government. The president is the elected chief of state, assisted by a prime minister and civilian Council of

Ministers. Only the president can appoint or dismiss members of the council. The president is elected for a five-year term and appoints the prime minister to run the government. The National Assembly is the legislative branch of the government. It has 70 seats.

On the local government level, Rwanda is divided into 12 prefectures, or districts. Each prefecture is named after the town that serves as its administrative center: Butare, Byumba, Cyangugu, Gikongoro, Gisenyi, Gitarama, Kibungo, Kibuye, Kigali, Kigaliville, Ruhengeri, and Umutara. The president appoints a prefect to supervise each of these districts.

Rwanda's legal system follows Belgian procedures and precedents set up during the colonial period. Law is based on the constitution of 1991 and, to a certain degree, on tribal custom. The president appoints judges to the Constitutional Court, which has two branches: the Council of State and the Court of Cassation. These two branches oversee various lower courts. Lower courts include a general, first trial court (called a court of first instance) in each prefecture, courts of appeal in Kigali, Ruhengeri, and Nyabisindu, and police courts in the towns and villages. In some of the most remote and least populated areas, cantonal (also called communal) courts dispense justice according to tribal law. Both police and cantonal courts try only minor cases, such as theft.

Rwanda's defense consists of a small army and an even smaller air force. There is no navy. Military manpower totals around 62,000. Rwanda has no draft or compulsory military service, so all soldiers are volunteers. Most of them are Hutu. The president serves as defense minister and commander-in-chief of the armed forces.

**Two Rwandan children pose for the camera on their way to school in Kigali. Rwanda's young and rapidly growing population is an ethnic mix of Hutu, Tutsi, and Twa.**

# 5

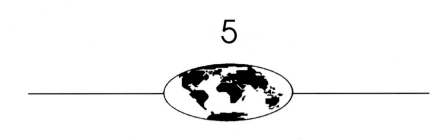

# The People of Rwanda

About 7,957,000 people live in Rwanda, giving the country an average population density of 760 people per square mile (293 per square kilometer). This makes Rwanda the most densely populated country in Africa, as well as one of the 25 most densely populated nations in the world. Such high density occurs because most Rwandans live only in areas suited for farming.

The most densely populated regions are the northern Great Rift Valley, the high lava plains south of the Virunga Mountains, the western Congo-Nile Crest, and the central plateaus. Some prime agricultural areas are severely overcrowded with well over 1,500 people per square mile (577 per square kilometer). Few people live in the mountain areas where farming conditions are poor.

Although most Rwandans live in rural areas, many have migrated to Kigali to find work. Kigali is Rwanda's capital city, located in the central plateau region. It is also Rwanda's most developed area, with a population of about 170,000. Other relatively urban centers, with fewer than 35,000 inhabitants, are Butare, southwest of Kigali, and Gisenyi and Ruhengeri in the northwest.

Rwanda is one of Africa's fastest-growing countries. Its population is increasing at a rate of about 4 percent per year. The high birth rate adds to the problems of overcrowding. The Rwandan government has not yet developed policies or programs for birth control, so Rwandans continue to have large extended families.

Rwandans still speak Kinyarwanda, an ancient Bantu language. Kinyarwanda, French, and English are the official languages of Rwanda. Most educated Rwandans speak two languages, but the uneducated speak only Kinyarwanda, the language of their forefathers. Because society was traditionally based on cattle raising, words and phrases relating to cattle make up a large part of Kinyarwanda. Some Rwandans in the border areas also speak Swahili.

Almost every Rwandan belongs to one of three distinct ethnic groups—Hutu, Tutsi, or Twa. These three groups have lived together uneasily for centuries. Long before the first Europeans came to Rwanda, a well-developed feudal system was functioning, with the Tutsi minority as the overlords of the Hutu farmers and Twa hunters.

These three groups share a common language and culture, even though they have been divided by geographical and historical differences. In the decades since Rwanda gained independence, divisions between the Twa, Hutu, and Tutsi began to blur as members of the three groups interacted socially and even intermarried. But the civil war and genocide in the beginning of the 1990s set back any true understanding between these groups.

The Hutu (also known as the Bahutu) are Rwanda's largest ethnic group, accounting for 80 percent of the population. They are a stocky and muscular people. The average adult male is about five feet, five inches (1.7 meters) tall and weighs 130 pounds (59 kilograms). The Hutu are descended from Bantu tribes who lived north of the equator, and are closely related to other groups of Bantu descendants living in neighboring Burundi, Tanzania, Uganda, and Democratic Republic of the Congo (Zaire).

Traditionally, the Hutu have been Rwanda's farmers. Before the political uprising that led to Rwanda's independence, they were the social inferiors of the Tutsi overlords in Rwanda's feudal system. After independence, however, the Hutu gained control of

**A young boy models his wool sweater as two traditionally dressed boys look on.**

Rwanda's government. They began to make great economic progress with many Hutu holding prominent positions in business as well as in government.

Traditional Hutu clothing was made from plain, handwoven cloth. The basic style was a sleeved shirt worn over a knee-length kilt. Most Hutu wore this outfit when working on the farms. When celebrating, Hutu dancers wore colorful, showy garments and feather headdresses.

The Tutsi (also known as the Watutsi or the Batutsi) are Rwanda's second largest ethnic group, making up about 19 percent of the country's population. This figure has decreased of course, as many Tutsi have left Rwanda to escape the terror of 1994 or were killed in the massacre. Some have resettled in Burundi, which is ruled by the Tutsi but most of the refugees have recently returned to try to live in their native land. More than half of the Tutsi in Rwanda live in the central plateau region around Nyanza, the former capital of the Tutsi kings.

Compared with the Hutu and the Twa, the Tutsi are fairly tall and thin, with lighter skin and more angular features. Their average weight is about 125 pounds (57 kilograms) and their average height is about five feet, nine inches (1.5 meters, 23 centimeters), though some Tutsi are well over six feet (1.8 meters) tall.

These taller Tutsi are the descendants of the famous dancers of the former royal court of Rwanda. The dancers won worldwide acclaim for their striking features and exciting dances. They wore colorful costumes of red, white, yellow, green, and gold cloth as

60

well as leopard-skin kilts. Long strands of beads, streaming feather headdresses, and small strings of bells around the ankles added to their pageantry. The dancers held small bows or long, light spears to symbolize their warrior heritage.

Traditionally, the Tutsi nobility wore ankle-length, cloak like garments draped over one shoulder. A simple but brightly colored pattern was often woven into the fabric. Ankle and wrist bracelets were also worn.

The Tutsi are descended from nomadic cattle herdsmen and warriors from the Nile River basin who settled in Rwanda about 500 years ago. During the centuries before independence, the Tutsi controlled Rwandan society. They held almost all government positions and owned most of the land and cattle. After independence, they lost power to the Hutu.

The Twa (also known as the Batwa) have been in Rwanda longer than any other group. At one time they were the largest group in Rwanda. Now they make up about 1 percent of the population. The Twa are descended from certain tribes of Pygmies, the first people known to have lived in east central Africa. They are a small people, averaging slightly over five feet (one and a half meters) in height.

Like the Pygmies, the Twa have always preferred to live in the forest. Traditionally, they lived by hunting and gathering wild foods. When the Hutu came to Rwanda and began turning forests into farmland, the number of Twa began to decrease. Later, as the Tutsi gained dominance, the Twa found a place in Rwandan society. Many of them settled near the Tutsi royal courts, although some bands remained in the western mountain forests. They served the Tutsi nobility as dancers, court jesters, guards, and sometimes as spies and executioners.

When the Tutsi lost power, the Twa lost their social status. Today, they are considered outsiders by the Hutu majority, who look down on traditional Twa customs and practices. Some Twa still live in Rwanda's few remaining forests. Others live near Hutu and Tutsi settlements, where most of them work as potters and other artisans.

Besides the Hutu, Tutsi, and Twa, Rwanda's population includes members of other ethnic groups. A small number of Hima nomads wander the northeastern plains. These nomads are distantly related to the Tutsi. They also originated in the Nile River basin and raised cattle. According to ancient legend, the Hima once owned all of Rwanda. But their evil behavior angered the gods, who took the land away from them. Today, they are considered bad omens and outcasts in Rwandan society.

Several thousand Europeans and Asians also live in Rwanda. The Europeans—more than 60 percent of whom are Belgian—work as missionaries, teachers, and business or government administrators. Most Asians in Rwanda—Indians, Pakistanis, and Arabs—run small businesses, although some work in technical and clerical positions in the government. A few United States citizens live in Rwanda. Almost all of them are involved in private business.

(continued on page 71)

# Scenes of

## RWANDA

A shared wood-burning brick oven provides baked goods for this village's population.

Traditional and Western-style clothing mix on the busy streets of Kigali.

Children orphaned during the massacre in 1994 stand in line at a refugee camp for food.

The minaret of an Islamic mosque looms over the Muslim quarter of Kigali.

Small, tin-roofed houses crowd the hills overlooking a Kigali car wash.

This primitive forge for iron hoes is a striking example of Rwanda's lack of industrial development.

Large, flat-bottomed barges transport materials across Rwanda's many lakes.

A woman balances a mat and the goods she hopes to sell at a nearby market.

Rwanda's northern mountains are home to a depleting gorilla population.

**Flowering plants brighten the forested hills.**

**A Rwandan farmer harvests his crop of potatoes without the aid of machinery.**

Aid workers inspect a fish pond built with foreign development funds.

Intensive cultivation has deforested and eroded Rwanda's landscape.

A guide leads the way up a path to the summit of Mt. Karasimbi.

In Rwanda, as in most agricultural societies, life revolves around the extended family, or clan. Family heritage determines one's social status and place of residence. Bloodlines are meticulously recorded, and every person is part of several large clans.

Most Rwandans live in family compounds scattered throughout the countryside in the most fertile areas. In these compounds, known as *rugos*, smaller houses surround the main family homestead, or *kraal*. As the family grows, new houses are built. The houses, built in the traditional central African beehive shape, are made of thatch, which is covered with a mixture of clay and cattle dung that provides strength and insulation. The entire compound is fenced in by young trees and branches lashed together. The family uses the land outside the fence for farming and raising livestock. The animals are usually brought into the rugo at night to protect them from thieves and wild animals. Almost every family member helps with planting, harvesting, and raising livestock.

The traditional nuclear family of father, mother, and children forms the basic family unit. Polygamy—the taking of more than one wife—was once very common but is now outlawed. Often, the nuclear family includes other relatives, such as an elderly grandparent, aunt, or uncle. Family ties are so strong that almost no one lives alone. A new widow or orphan is immediately taken in by relatives and becomes part of the family.

In Rwandan families, the father is the unquestioned head of the household. Family members must obey him in all matters. In the past, the father had the right to kill any member of this family

71

**Her child strapped to her back, a woman goes shopping in an open-air market.**

who disobeyed him or brought dishonor to the family name. Although this practice is now forbidden by law, absolute respect for the father is still a part of Rwandan family life. Even today, a father may prohibit his children from saying his name.

Many women have ten or more children and raising them is the mother's responsibility. Mother and child are inseparable until the child is about two years old. A mother carries her young child in a sling on her back and older children ride on her hip. Almost all children are breastfed, often until age three or four, or until the mother becomes pregnant again. Boys and girls are raised alike until they are four or five years old. The girls then learn how to do the household chores, and the boys learn how to farm and tend the livestock.

Almost from birth, a child is taught the rules, myths, rituals, and traditions of the family and society. Parents teach their children respect for elders, politeness, generosity, and cooperation. Unlike many other African societies, Rwanda has few formal rituals to mark the passage from childhood to puberty.

Aside from the nuclear family, the most important social group in Rwanda has traditionally been the *inzu*. An inzu is a loosely organized extended family made up of four or five generations on the father's side. All the members may live together in one *rugo* or, if it is a large inzu, in adjoining compounds. The head of the inzu, the *umukungu,* is chosen by the all members. He settles all disputes, punishes clan members who have committed crimes, and represents the inzu in dealing with the government and other clans.

Other, larger kin groups in Rwanda include *umuryangos*, groups of inzus that share a common lineage. There are also *ubwokos*, huge extended clans loosely tied together by shared ancestors.

These traditional kin groups were once vital to Rwanda's social structure, especially in the days of Tutsi royal rule. But social and political changes over the last several decades have made clan relationships less important. In particular, land shortage makes it more difficult for sons to settle on their fathers' rugos. New families often have to move to other areas of Rwanda where land is available.

Today, a more important social unit is the *umuhana*, a kind of closeknit neighborhood group. A typical umuhana has several nuclear families who live near each other. The group's members may or may not be related, but they all cooperate and support each other as if they were. They help each other in farming, herding, building houses, and economic matters, and as a group perform religious ceremonies and deal with government authorities.

Despite the recent changes in Rwandan society, old traditions and customs endure. Elaborate rituals, particularly for the birth of a child and his or her naming, marriage, and death, mark the life of every person. Families celebrate these rituals together, which keep family ties strong. Many of these rituals are linked to the people's religious belief in the spirit world of gods and sacred ancestors.

Rwanda's constitution guarantees freedom of religion, and worship plays an important role in the life of almost every Rwandan. Christianity, mainly Roman Catholicism, was brought to Rwanda by European missionaries in the late 19th century. Christianity quickly gained widespread acceptance because of its similarities to many tribal rites—and because the missionaries built hospitals and schools to help improve the quality of Rwandan life. Today, more than five million Catholics and 720,000 Protestants—a total of 75 percent of the population—call themselves Christians. A small but growing number of Rwandans practice Islam, and there are tiny communities of Hindus and Buddhists. About half of Rwanda's people practice traditional religions.

In rural areas, these traditional beliefs have blended with elements of Christian religions. At the core of this worship is *Imana*—an omnipresent, almighty being who creates and preserves all life. He and a number of lesser spirits protect and guide Rwandans in their daily lives. The popular saying *"Imana Y'i Rwanda"* (Rwanda is Imana's country), and the old proverb, "If Imana is out walking elsewhere during the day, he will come home at night to Rwanda," show how strongly the people rely on their belief in Imana. His name is used in naming children, in blessings and oaths, and during marriage and burial ceremonies.

Traditional tribal religion also holds that every human, animal, and object possesses a life force that is also called *imana*. The belief that animals or objects have a life force and a self-awareness is called animism. According to these beliefs, the spiritual force disappears when an animal dies. But when a human dies, his imana is transformed into *abazimu*, a malicious spirit of the dead that hovers around the family compound.

Abazimu brings bad luck and misfortune—epidemics of cattle diseases, crop failures, and sickness—to its clan, whose life and possessions it envies. To counteract this evil force, the clan consults a witch doctor, or *umufumu*, to learn why the abazimu is angry and how to satisfy it. Elaborate rituals designed to show respect and admiration help to calm the evil spirit.

Eventually, abazimu loses the human's personal identity and maliciousness. It then becomes an honored, positive energy force in the spirit world. Families pray to these sacred ancestral spirits and consult them on important matters.

The most powerful member of Rwanda's ancestral spirit world is *Ryangombe*. The *babandwa*, a special religious fraternity with its own secret and complicated membership rules, holds a festival every July to worship Ryangombe. During the festival, the members of the babandwa paint their faces and bodies and decorate spirit huts. A member of the group is made up to appear as Ryangombe himself, carrying his sacred spear. After an elaborate ritual of chanting, dancing, and drumming, the babandwa members purify themselves by washing in a stream.

One Hutu ritual involves the belief that smooth, round stones found in streams contain the power of Imana and bring good fortune to their possessor. Family members collect several stones and place them in a small hut, or *ndaro*, just outside of the rugo. They then bring the stones daily offerings of beer, milk, meat, and other gifts to please Imana.

Priests conduct the various rituals and ceremonies and act as mediators between humans and the spirits. They have the power to speak to the spirits, foretell the future, and, with the proper offerings, ask the gods for favors. The local priest is one of the most powerful men in every Rwandan community. A priest usually inherits his position from his father, although sometimes a man is seized by a spirit and given the power to communicate with and influence the spirit world.

Witch doctors, or *abafumu* (the plural of *umufumu*), are believed to have powers to communicate with the dead and protect the living from misfortune caused by the evil abazimu or by witches. Abafumu act as healers, using various plant and herbal preparations and sacred charms to treat illness. Most Rwandans still consult their local abafumu before seeking modern medical care. Abafumu also interpret dreams, call together spirits in secret seances, and predict the future. Their special equipment and clothing—a gourd rattle, leopard-skin cape, and cowtail headdress—are considered sacred. Abafumu pass them, along with secret incantations and curing techniques, to their sons or young apprentices.

Abafumu can also identify a witch, or *abarosi*, and protect people from harm caused by the witch's spells. Abarosi are held responsible for all kinds of misfortune, from major disasters such as death and crop failure to minor mishaps such as a stubbed toe or a leaky roof. They practice "contagious" magic, using items from a person's body, perhaps a lock of hair or fingernail clippings, to gain power over the person's soul. Anyone found guilty of practicing witchcraft is beaten and driven from the community.

Most Rwandans, even those converted to Christianity, recognize certain taboos, or *imiziro*. The imiziro range from major social taboos such as incest to various restrictions on what a person can eat. For example, many Rwandans will not eat chicken or eggs, or drink milk. Other imiziro include the beliefs that if a woman whistles her husband will die, and that if a pregnant woman looks upon a white man or hears a gunshot, her child will suffer.

Everyone rejoices when a child is born, and boys and girls are equally cherished. A boy helps keep the clan powerful, and a girl will someday bring a dowry, or bride-price, when she marries. Twins, or impanga, are believed to be the offspring of a woman and a god. As a result, they are considered the gods' favorites. Parents perform special rituals to prevent the gods from taking their twins back to the spirit world. Yet impanga are also seen as bad omens, and their birth makes the whole community uneasy.

Most children are born at home with the help of neighbors and a local midwife. Right after birth, the infant is bathed in cold water and rubbed all over with butter to protect it from evil spirits. This practice is continued every day for the first six months of

**The government hopes that Rwandans will limit their families to only two children.**

the baby's life. To further protect the child from evil spirits, the placenta is buried under the bed and the umbilical cord is kept as an amulet (Rwandans believe that if someone's umbilical cord is lost, great harm will come to that person). After six days, neighbors and relatives bring gifts for the new baby and the mother.

Like many undeveloped countries, Rwanda has a tragically high death rate among infants. For this reason, a father waits three to four months before naming the new baby, until he is sure it will survive. He chooses the name carefully, for Rwandans believe that a person's name has a great effect on his or her life. A child's name

78

reflects the family background and the father's hopes and dreams for his child. The father also gives the child some nicknames, for many believe that harm comes to a person called by his real name.

The child's paternal grandfather presides at the naming ceremony. With all the family gathered around, he gives the child a personal name to go with his clan name. He anoints the child's feet and hands and explains the reasons for the child's name. If the family practices Christianity, a formal baptism may follow. The naming ceremony ends with a feast, at which relatives and friends give gifts to the newly named baby, who is now a full-fledged member of society.

Rwandan fathers often arrange their children's marriages. If a young man wishes to marry a young woman not chosen for him, he must have his father's approval. Marriage between Hutu and Tutsi used to be very rare, but it has become more acceptable in the last 20 years or so.

Before the marriage takes place, the boy's family must pay a dowry to the girl's family. This payment, usually in the form of cattle, goats, or hoes and other farm tools, makes the marriage official. Often, the larger the dowry a young man can offer, the better his chance of gaining the approval of the girl's father.

On the wedding day, or *bukwe*, a procession leaves the groom's house bearing wedding gifts and the dowry. The procession stops at the bride's front door. At first, the bride pretends to cry and resists leaving her home, but when she sees the gifts she happily joins the procession.

At the wedding ceremony, or *kurongora*, the bride is blessed and crowned with flowers. She is then formally introduced to the groom's family. A feast follows, with much singing, dancing, and beer drinking. The bride's family is not part of the celebration, although they send gifts. In Rwanda, when a woman marries, she becomes part of her husband's family and leaves her own family behind. The new couple usually lives in or near the husband's father's rugo.

Although marriage is revered by Rwandans, divorce is surprisingly common and easy to obtain. A simple ritual known as *gutana* ends a marriage without elaborate formal procedures or court hearings. If a dissatisfied husband wants to end a marriage, he merely sends his wife back to her family. If it is the wife's choice, she leaves her husband's house. The wife's family usually tries to reconcile the couple because they will have to return the dowry if the marriage ends. But if all attempts at reconciliation fail, gutana is final.

Gift giving is an important part of almost every occasion, not just marriage. Long after the wedding, the husband often gives gifts to his wife's family. When the bride's mother comes to visit her daughter, she usually brings a small gift. Relatives and friends bring gifts to a new mother and her baby, both after birth and at the naming ceremony. And most business transactions are sealed with an exchange of gifts.

One of the most common gifts is beer, which is drunk at all social occasions, including weddings, funerals, and everyday visits. Any visitor to a Rwandan household is immediately offered beer as a sign of hospitality and friendship. Refusing to drink is a serious insult to the host. But a Rwandan will refuse to drink with anyone who has wronged him or who has done something disrespectful.

Many people brew their own beer at home from bananas, millet, sorghum, or honey. The beer is traditionally served in a large clay pot. Each person drinks from the pot through his own straw, usually made from a hollow reed.

*Urupfu,* the funeral rituals, play a vital role in the life of a family, keeping it solid and strong when it has lost a member. Rwandans believe that a person's soul lives on after death and that the spirit continues to participate in family life. The family rugo usually has a spirit house, a small building that houses the ancestral spirits. The family's dead are all buried near the spirit house to help keep the family strong.

When a person dies, his family stops all work. Neighbors and relatives bring food and firewood and do all the chores while the family prepares for the funeral. Before burial, the corpse is rubbed with butter and placed in a crouching position, with the arms and legs tied together. Both these rituals are intended to prevent the dead person's spirit from reentering the body.

At the funeral, female family members shave their heads and, with much wailing and crying, try to prevent the body from being buried. After the burial, the whole family enters a period of mourning, which may last several months. During mourning, family members refuse to eat salt and stop all life-giving activities, including sexual relations and the planting of crops.

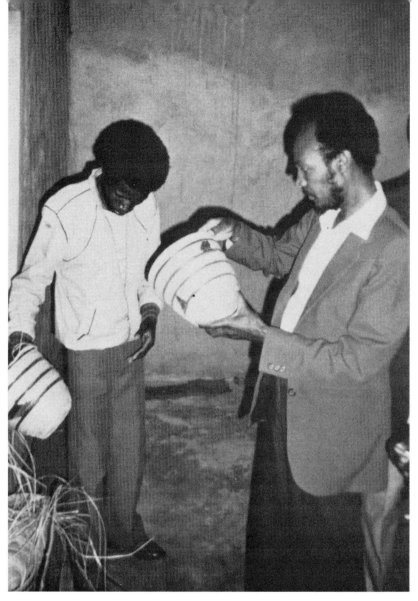

Two men admire handwoven Rwandan baskets, which are renowned for their beauty and durability. The number of baskets in a home indicates the owner's social standing.

# 6

# Artistic Traditions

Rwanda's rich artistic heritage includes music, dance, oral literature, and crafts. The traditional arts are still practiced and play an important role in keeping old customs alive.

Rwanda's traditional arts are the products of intense religious beliefs and customs. Most art serves as part of the ceremonies and rituals directed toward the spirit world. Rwandans, through music, dance, and stories, have traditionally expressed and celebrated the moral and religious convictions that shape their lives.

Music plays an important role in the daily lives of all Rwandans. Ritual ceremonies associated with birth, death, marriage, harvest, hunting, and many other events include singing, dancing, and instrumental music.

Almost everyone is involved in music in some way. Some play instruments, while others sing, dance, or clap along with the rhythm. Travelers and visitors traditionally brought news from afar by chanting songs around their hosts' fires.

Although the distinctions have gradually blurred over time, each Rwandan ethnic group has its own distinctive musical style.

The Hutu have many songs for special occasions such as harvesting, hunting, and beer drinking.

Traditional Tutsi songs center on cattle herding. There are special songs for watering the cattle, driving them home for the evening, showing them to a guest, and selling a cow or a bull. Other old Tutsi songs glorify past wars and conquests.

Twa songs are mostly about hunting. In the days of the Tutsi feudal monarchy, the Twa often served as court entertainers, singing bawdy and satirical songs for the enjoyment of the Tutsi chiefs and their families.

The Belgian colonial administration and the Christian missionaries discouraged many of these traditional songs. Some songs were even banned. Despite recent efforts to record and preserve them, many old songs have been lost or forgotten.

Traditional African instruments create astonishing varieties of sound and rhythm. The most popular and typically African instrument used in Rwanda is the drum, which comes in a great number of shapes and sizes. Today, drums are used almost exclusively for music; in the past, they were used to send messages over long distances.

Before the overthrow of the Tutsi monarchy, the mwami's court was the center for musical education and composition. The Royal Drummers, a group that gained widespread fame both within and outside of Africa, dominated the court. The *kalinga* (a sacred drum) was the symbol of the mwami's power and a source of spiritual energy. The kalinga was kept hidden and brought out only for special occasions and ceremonies, such as the Tutsi dances.

84

Drummers often play in groups. A full drum "orchestra" has seven to nine drums ranging in tone from low to high. The basic rhythm is usually set by the smallest drum, called the soprano drum, which has the highest tone. The other drums—tenor, alto, baritone, bass, and double bass—back up the soprano, often with very intricate rhythmic patterns. As many as three or four patterns may be played at once, creating a unique, complex sound.

Other popular instruments are the *mbira*, or thumb piano (also called a *kalimba*), the *lulunga*, and flutes made from hollow stems and reeds. The mbira, widely used throughout central Africa,

**A Tutsi dancer poses in traditional feathered headdress and kilt. The two spears are used in the dance.**

consists of several narrow, curved metal strips attached to a small board or box. The metal pieces are plucked with the thumb to produce soft, haunting melodies. People walking along the road often keep themselves company by playing the mbira. The lulunga, an eight-stringed instrument that resembles a harp, is often used as the background music for singing or dancing. Sometimes it provides a melodic counterpoint to drums.

Drums and other instruments provide music for dancers. Rwandan dancing is very complex, as intricate in movement as any classical ballet. Traditional Tutsi dances celebrate cattle and war. The most frequently performed Hutu dances celebrate events such as births, weddings, and successful harvests. Most Rwandans dance informally at clan gatherings and religious rites.

Rwanda has a rich oral literary tradition of myths, fables, folk tales, poetry, and proverbs. Public speaking is a respected form of artistic expression, and most Rwandans take great pride in the way they express themselves. A good storyteller is always a welcome guest in any home.

Many of the popular myths and folk tales convey a moral or message. Favorite themes include the unpredictable and often malicious ways of the spirits, the ways crafty heroes use their wits to outsmart brutal enemies, and the value of cooperation and generosity. This rich store of oral literature transmits the traditional values from generation to generation. Rwanda has no written literary tradition because relatively few Rwandans can read and write.

Rwandan crafts are practical as well as decorative. Most artwork takes the form of useful household objects. Artisans paint woven reed room dividers, mats, baskets, and other items with intricate geometrical patterns. Most designs are in black and white, but red is sometimes added. There is also some wood carving, mainly of drums, smoking pipes, stools, knife handles, and scabbards. Wooden bowls and jugs are often given simple carved decorations that also designate ownership.

In Rwanda, baskets are a sign of wealth and status; the number and quality of baskets sometimes shows a family's social standing. Basket weaving is a very important craft, both for its practical purpose and for the artistic outlet it provides for the women of Rwanda. Weavers use the sticky fibers of papyrus, banana, and other plants to create high-quality, waterproof baskets, used as cups and bowls, storage containers of all types and sizes, coiled rings for carrying burdens on top of the head, and even holders for beer pots.

Generally, the natural fibers of the baskets dry to shades of tan and yellow. The basket-makers then weave in strips of dyed fibers, usually in black and shades of purple and red, to make geometric patterns. Popular design elements include zigzags, triangles, squares, rectangles, and spirals. Some of the more formal designs use white and blue beads. The most common design is banana leaves, representing the importance of the banana tree and its fruit.

Rwanda's economy is primarily based on individual labor without the benefit of modern tools and transportation. The man above has shaped these earthen bricks by hand.

# 7

# The Struggle for
# Development

Despite attempts at economic improvement, Rwanda remains one
of the world's poorest countries. Education, health care, and other
social welfare programs have also lagged. About 90 percent of the
rural population and 30 percent of the urban population lives in
poverty. In 1996, the yearly per capita income was equal to U.S.
$440. Rwanda's basic economic problems stem from a shortage of
fertile land, overpopulation, and lack of transportation. Also the
civil war that occurred in the first half of the 1990s set the country back considerably.

Rwanda has a free-market economy, which means that the government does not control the economy. The unit of currency is
the Rwanda franc (in January 1998, 302 Rwandan francs equaled
one U.S. dollar). The European Union is Rwanda's main source
of foreign aid along with the United States. Most of this aid goes
toward agriculture, education, telecommunications, and health

care. Other important sources of foreign economic aid include the United Nations, France, Germany, Switzerland, and Canada.

Agriculture supports about 93 percent of Rwanda's people. Most crops are grown on small family farms and are eaten by the people who raise them. This is known as subsistence farming. The major food crops grown for local consumption are beans and peas, sweet potatoes, cassava (a vegetable root), potatoes, corn, sorghum, millet and other cereal grains, and groundnuts. These crops grow well even in poor, densely planted soil. They can also be stored as food reserves if a new harvest fails. Sorghum and millet are fermented for beer and are combined with corn to make flour for baking or porridge. Bananas are Rwanda's traditional basic crop because they grow year-round and are very versatile.

Farmers eat them fresh, ferment them to make beer, and sell what they do not use.

Rwanda's important cash crops (those sold for export) are coffee, tea, cotton, and pyrethrum, a flower used to make insecticides. These account for more than 80 percent of Rwanda's export revenues each year.

Coffee is the country's chief cash crop. About one-half of the country is suitable for coffee-growing, but the best growing zones are near Lake Kivu and in the center of the country near Kigali. Rwanda's premium coffee, coffea arabica, commands a high price on world markets, but farmers can grow only small amounts. Government programs to introduce higher-yielding trees and to teach farmers better cultivation methods are raising production.

**Terraced hillsides are a common sight in the Rwandan countryside.**

Tea is another important cash crop, because it can be grown in most Rwandan soils. It is also easy to ship, something especially important to a country with no railroads or seaports. Tea production has grown rapidly in the last three decades, and the government is encouraging more tea cultivation.

Pyrethrum, a small, daisy-like flower, thrives in Rwanda's volcanic soils. Its flowers are dried and used to make a natural insecticide. The pyrethrum grown in Rwanda is some of the finest in the world.

Rwandans once depended heavily on cattle for milk, butter, and other dairy products; the number of cattle a person owned was also a sign of wealth and prestige. But cattle have lost much of their economic importance, largely because of overgrazing. Now there are more cattle than can be supported on the available pastureland. This causes serious overgrazing, which depletes the already sparse grasses and eventually leads to soil erosion. The herds of long-horned Ankole and Renga cattle do not get enough to eat, and thin cattle are of little commercial value for beef, milk. or butter. Because smaller, healthier herds would be more beneficial to the country, the government wants farmers to keep fewer cattle.

Disease greatly diminishes the economic value of cattle as well. Although new vaccines are helping to control some animal diseases, almost half of all cattle in Rwanda have tapeworm, an intestinal parasite that prevents the cattle from being sold for human consumption. Almost one-third of the cattle die from sleeping sickness, a disease carried by tsetse flies. These flies breed by the millions in Rwanda's marshlands. Government efforts to control the tsetse fly by clearing swamp vegetation and spraying have had limited success.

Rwandan farmers raise other livestock—sheep, goats, pigs, rabbits. and chickens are found on most farms. The farmland shortage also affects these animals, however, and they are of little economic importance. Most are raised for use by the farmers themselves, not for commercial sale.

Despite its great number of farms, Rwanda is plagued by hunger. The land cannot feed its people because of the unfavorable climate, with months of heavy rain followed by periods of extreme drought, the shortage of arable land, overcrowding, and poor farming methods.

Rwanda's hilly terrain and scattered farms make tractors and other farm machinery impractical. Even the use of ox-drawn plows, a traditional method of cultivation in Africa, is difficult in most parts of Rwanda. As a result, fields are usually planted by hand, using small, heart-shaped iron hoes. Crops are harvested by hand as well, using the serpette (a small, sharp sickle attached to a short handle) and the adz (a machete-like tool).

In an effort to mechanize farms and ease overcrowding at the same time, the government created a new type of farm known as the paysannat. Paysannats are planned agricultural communities consisting of several privately owned plots organized for maximum productivity.

Traditional family farms, which typically consist of small scattered plots on less than four acres (one and a half hectares) are difficult to cultivate. But paysannats have larger fields, averaging more than six acres (two and a half hectares) of land. The fields are laid out along a central access road. Homesteads are built along the road, next to the main cash-crop fields. This layout allows for better transportation and for the mechanization of certain farm activities, such as spraying insecticides and harvesting. It also helps with the introduction of new farming methods. Each paysannat grows a particular cash crop, usually coffee. Pyrethrum, tea, and cotton are also grown. Most paysannats are located in south central Rwanda. Others are being developed in the Ruzizi Valley in Rwanda's southwestern corner.

The government is also trying to reduce soil erosion, another major problem. Erosion, caused by heavy rainfall on overcrowded, poorly managed farmland, washes the fertile topsoil from the hillsides. With poorer soil, farms become less productive. By teaching farmers to rotate their crops (to plant different crops each year on the same soil) and to plant trees and hedges that will hold the soil in place, the government hopes to reduce erosion and save Rwanda's best farmland. It is also attempting to develop new farmland by draining eastern swamp lands and irrigating dry regions of the savannas.

Introducing new food and cash crops is another important way of boosting agricultural productivity. With Belgian aid, some modern peanut farms were started in the eastern part of the country. Taiwan helped Rwandan farmers plant rice on plots of marshland where little else will grow. Soybeans and sugarcane are also being tried as cash crops.

94

Industry has come slowly or not at all to Rwanda. Despite gradual industrial expansion after 1962, less than 2 percent of the work force holds manufacturing jobs. There are only a small number of manufacturing plants in Rwanda. Private investment in Rwandan industry is low. In recent decades, violence between the Hutu and the Tutsi has discouraged prospective investors.

Several other problems hold back industrial growth. Because few people have the money to buy manufactured goods, it is difficult to create a domestic market for industrial products. Rwanda's lack of transportation restricts export markets because it is difficult to get products to ports or customers. Also, Rwanda has few skilled laborers because most Rwandans work only on farms.

Although Rwanda has enormous potential for energy production, it has not been able to harness that energy to power its factories. Many rivers and streams could be good sources of hydroelectric power, and the large deposits of methane gas in the depths of Lake Kivu could supply power for factories. But most of this potential remains untapped, mainly because there is not enough money to build dams and power plants to exploit these natural sources of energy. In 1977, Rwanda, Tanzania, and Burundi did join to exploit the hydroelectric and mineral potential of the Kagera River basin. But Rwanda still imports much of the energy it uses.

Despite these problems, some industries have developed in Rwanda. The most rapid growth has occurred in food processing and textiles. Other industries have been established in wood, paint, soap, and furniture. Europeans and Asians own most manufacturing plants; many of the rest are run as cooperatives (the workers own the plant). Very few native Rwandans own private firms.

Most large manufacturing plants are located in the capital city of Kigali, but small-scale factories are scattered around the country. Kigali has shoe and clothing factories, a farm-tool factory, coffee and tea processing plants, small plants that produce soap, paints, and rabies and smallpox vaccines, and two small factories where electronic components are assembled.

Other areas of Rwanda have flourishing cottage industries—the making of small articles by skilled craftsmen and artisans in their

**A worker sorts newly forged hoes by hand in one of Rwanda's few factories.**

**The international airport at Kanombe.**

homes or workshops. Important cottage industry products include baskets, pottery, furniture, and bricks.

Despite Rwanda's rich mineral deposits, mining plays a relatively minor role in the economy. It does, however, account for about 20 percent of Rwanda's exports. Tin is the most important mineral export, followed by tungsten and beryl. Clay, sand, gravel, lime, and building stone are mined for use within Rwanda. Most exports are sent to countries in the European Union and the United States. The Rwandan government hopes to decrease its dependence on Belgium by building a tin foundry near Kigali with the help of a loan from the European Investment Bank. Today, Rwanda produces just over one percent of the world's tin.

Despite the natural beauty of Rwanda's Kagera National Park, National Park of the Volcanoes, and other areas, tourism remains an underdeveloped industry in Rwanda especially due to all the

97

recent unrest in the area. The country's only popular resort is Gisenyi, on the shore of Lake Kivu.

Roads are virtually the only means of commercial transportation in Rwanda. The country's many rivers are unsuitable for commercial navigation; only Lake Kivu can handle freighters, but

**Although education is free, many Rwandan students drop out of school.**

traffic is limited. There are no railways. Lack of transportation has severely hurt Rwanda's economic development.

Rwanda continues to rely heavily on its fairly well-developed road system. Five main roads connect Kigali with Kagitumba, Kibungo, Gisenyi, Gatuna, and Cyangugu. Major roads link Rwanda with the neighboring countries of Burundi, Uganda,

Tanzania, and the Democratic Republic of the Congo (Zaire). Most of Rwanda's imports and exports travel by truck along a 1,000-mile (1,609-kilometer) road through Uganda and Kenya to or from the Indian Ocean seaport of Mombasa, on Kenya's southeastern coast. Another important trade route runs south by road through Burundi, then east by rail through Tanzania to the Port of Dar es Salaam.

Very few Rwandans own cars. Most use public or privately owned buses and taxis for travel within the country. Many still walk from their farms to market, the women carrying goods and produce on top of their heads.

Rwanda has an international airport just outside of Kigali. In the aftermath of the civil war internal flights in Rwanda have been suspended.

Like most developing countries, Rwanda has little in the way of modern communications systems. For instance, it has the fewest number of telephones per person in the world. It has only two radio stations, which broadcast mainly in French, and one television station.

Rwanda does, however, have a well-organized postal system. Mail service both within the country and overseas is fast and efficient.

Rwanda's newspapers were closed down during the civil war in the 1990s and as of 1997 had not resumed operations.

After independence in 1962, the Rwandan government made a major effort to increase literacy and to improve general education for all the people. Primary and secondary schooling were expanded and upgraded. Students spend six years in primary school and six years in secondary school. Primary education is divided into two cycles: the premier, or literary, cycle of four years, which is taught in Kinyarwanda, and the two-year cycle, which is taught in French.

In 1963, the government and the Roman Catholic Dominican Order of Canada established the National University of Rwanda in Butare. The university offers degrees in medicine, natural sciences, social sciences, and education.

Primary and secondary education is free for all Rwandan children. Despite this the dropout rate remains high. Only 25 percent of students advance as far as the fourth grade, and fewer than 2 percent reach secondary school. Most students leave school to work full time on their family farms. Enrollment drops even further in higher education. Less than seven of every 1,000 secondary school graduates go on to study at the National University or at overseas institutions.

Like many other developing countries, Rwanda faces many public health problems. Among the most urgent are malnutrition, impure water, unsanitary living conditions, and inadequate medical care.

Malnutrition is Rwanda's most pressing health problem. The average Rwandan's diet contains too many starches, such as beans and sweet potatoes, and not enough fats and protein. Few people eat meat more than once or twice a month. Poor diet triggers a variety of medical disorders. Kwashiorkor, a severe form of malnutrition caused by lack of protein, is especially common in young children. Many children die from it, and many others develop liver disease and other health problems later in life.

Fewer than half the people have clean drinking water, and hardly any have modern indoor plumbing. Polluted drinking water and poor sanitation contribute to other serious diseases, especially malaria, dysentery, intestinal parasites, hepatitis, and tuberculosis.

The Ministry of Public Health oversees Rwanda's preventive-health and medical-treatment programs. Over the years, Rwanda has received much-needed assistance from Catholic and Protestant missionaries and from the Belgian government. Recently, other countries have provided health-care aid. The United States helped build a water-purification plant in Kigali, and France provided funds to build a hospital in Ruhengeri.

But the lack of funds and the shortage of hospitals, clinics, doctors, and nurses continue to plague Rwanda's public-health programs. And poverty still causes many Rwandan children to grow up unhealthy.

Men and women meet in a local church to discuss plans for their village. Such cooperation is needed to ensure Rwanda's economic and political development.

# 8

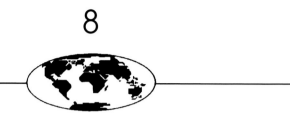

# Rwanda's Uncertain Future

Rwanda still faces many of the same problems it faced when independence was declared in 1962. Fervent cries of "independence," "freedom," and "one man, one vote," were heard throughout the country in 1962, as Rwandans rejoiced in self-government. But today the civil war torn country is struggling to survive. Refugees continue to pour back into the country and feeding and caring for them is a major task. The government has had to appeal to other countries for aid and food supplies numerous times in the past few years to try to stem the tide of starvation.

But while the ancient ethnic loyalties are stronger than loyalty to the nation Rwanda will remain one of the world's poorest nations, with uncertain prospects for economic growth, and unrest a way of life.

In addition to its own problems Rwanda is surrounded by countries that also have a great deal of political instability. Border disputes and continuing tribal tensions are everywhere.

**Rwanda's hopes for the future are children like these who have only recently returned to their villages from exile.**

Rwanda's government needs to use foreign aid to feed its people, build more and better roads, and improve health care. The nation is in dire need of communications networks, power stations, medical facilities, and schools to teach Rwandans basic skills, as well as more advanced work skills.

Educating Rwandans and creating these building blocks for economic progress will not be easy. Ethnic rivalries continue to divide the people. Rwanda's future depends on its people's ability to work together to achieve a healthier, more economically sound society for themselves and generations to come.

# GLOSSARY

| | |
|---|---|
| **abarosi** | A male or female witch whose spells are thought to cause crop failure, sterility, or death |
| **abazimu** | The ghost or evil spirit of a dead person, thought to bring bad fortune to its family |
| **Babandwa** | A religious fraternity with secret rituals. Its major festival is a celebration of the ancestral spirit |
| **bahinza** | The clan leader or king of the small Hutu kingdoms |
| **biru** | Honored members of the mwami's court who advised the king on tradition, tribal history, and spiritual matters |
| **bukwe** | Wedding day |
| **imana** | The supreme god of the traditional Rwandan religions |
| **imiziro** | Ritual taboos or forbidden acts. Some imiziro are forbidden foods, such as milk or eggs; others involve superstitions, such as if a woman whistles her husband will die |
| **kalinga** | A sacred drum, believed to be the source of the mwami's power and the country's spiritual energy, was used only for special festivals |

| | |
|---|---|
| **kraal** | The main homestead within a rugo, or family compound |
| **lulunga** | A harplike instrument with eight strings |
| **mbira** | A musical instrument made of a small board or box with narrow metal strips attached |
| **mwami** | The chief or king of Rwanda before independence. He was the head of an elaborate feudal system of chiefs, subchiefs, and clan leaders set up by the Tutsi |
| **paysannat** | A planned agricultural community in which homesteads are built along roads on previously unfarmed land; all of the individual farms in a paysannat grow the same cash crop |
| **pyrethrum** | A small, daisy-like flower that thrives in the volcanic soils of Rwanda's highest regions. Its dried flowers are used to make insecticides |
| **rugo** | A fenced or walled compound containing the houses of family members; a village |
| **ubwoko** | The largest family or clan structure |
| **umufunu** | A diviner or fortune-teller |
| **umuhana** | A social group made of several neighboring extended families who may or may not be related to one another |
| **umusozi** | "Hills," or subdivisions of the districts of the Rwandan kingdom. Each was ruled by a hill chief and divided into neighborhoods ruled by subchiefs |
| **urupfu** | Funeral rites |

# INDEX

PICTURE CREDITS

African Art Archives, pp. 35, 85; African Development Foundation, pp. 18, 23, 64 (above), 66-67 (above), 67 (below), 68-69 (below), 70 (above), 78, 82, 98-99, 103; African Wildlife Foundation, pp. 20, 27, 28, 68, 69; Africare, p.59; Associated Press, pp. 52, 65, 105; Dennis Degnan, pp 14, 56, 64, 65 (below), 66, 70 (below), 72, 88, 96, 97; Jason Lauré, pp. 68-69 (above), 90-91; New York Public Library, p. 37; Antonio M. Rossi, 17, 25, 63, 70 (below); UPI/Bettmann Newsphotos, 32, 39, 47, 49; U.S. Agency for International Development, p.44.